Crying Shame

Jeffrey Morgan

Crying Shame

Jeffrey Morgan

BlazeVOX [books]

Buffalo, New York

Crying Shame by Jeffrey Morgan

Book design by Geoffrey Gatza
Cover photo by Aaron M. Cohen
Author photo: Mitch Kern

First Edition
ISBN: 9781935402770
Library of Congress Control Number 2009910017

BlazeVOX [books]
303 Bedford Ave
Buffalo, NY 14216
Editor@blazevox.org

publisher of weird little books

BlazeVOX [books]

blazevox.org

2   4   6   8   0   9   7   5   3   1

BlazeVOX

Love and gratitude to my (poetry) teachers: Robin Becker, Diane Glancy, Alvin Greenberg, Julia Kasdorf, and especially Cecil Giscombe.

Love and gratitude to my parents John and Nancy Morgan for, among innumerable acts of generous parenting, encouraging me to do impractical things.

ACKNOWLEDGMENTS

Many thanks to the readers, editors, and staff of the following journals in which many of these poems first appeared, sometimes in different forms. I would especially like to say:

Anemone Sidecar: Thank you Kathryn Rantala

CanWeHaveOurBallBack: Thank you Jim Behrle

Cannibal: Thank you Matt and Katy Henriksen

DIAGRAM: Thank you Ander Monson

Fourteen Hills: Thank you Kristine Leja

Gumball: Thank you Ben Parzybok

La Petite Zine: Thank you Dan Nester

LIT: Thank you Mark Bibbins

Ocho: Thank you Meghan Punschke

Octopus: Thank you Zach Schomburg and Tony Tost

Pank: Thank you M. Bartley Seigel and Roxane Gay

Pavement Saw: Thank you David Baratier

PindeldyBoz: Thank you Mark Yakich

Spinning Jenny: Thank you C.E. Harrison

Unpleasant Event Schedule: Thanks again Dan Nester

And thank you again Ander Monson of the anthology *Diagram.2*.

For Carla

Table of Contents

Crying Shame

How Word Is Passed

How Word is Passed

I wake to prime numbers written in blue ink on my forearms.
The television's sparkling reflection selling in the glaze
Of her eyes the snow storm that will keep us.
How long have I been asleep?

I remember tendencies and sentiment of form:

"Words like pieces of topaz." Minutes/hours/days/years ago the glint
Of all of Eighth Street stocking up at Gristedes. Supple glare ringing off
White tile   shovel blades   excited teeth
Thinning to this deliberate process.

This is the shadow of the atomic bomb? Half-life moon. Seepage.
Sunlight coppering collar bones. My grandfather dropping
The star from our name: Morgenstern. Orange gears of horizon.
When someone says: *the double meaning of morning*.

We've been told things and so we tell others.

Nostalgia

Never ever fish your fingers into the garbage disposal,
no matter how sweetly it sings for your supper.
The tiny god in there, he is the deity of lawnmowers
and helicopters. Anything that spins sharp is his dominion.

Chainsaws, boat motors, sunflowers, youth.
He is more powerful and less sober than his reputation
which precedes him like cut fruit. You are him, he is you.
You are him doing his "you" impression.

He is not so much vengeful or arbitrary or mysterious
as he is half in the bag. There is a reason why
we say attention is something you pay.
We don't say: Dissection is the better part of clamor.

We don't say: You scream, I scream,
we all scream for nice dreams.

Work

I climb out of the refrigerator before dawn
and wipe the condensation from my spine.
It feels good to smell this fresh.

So I can speak softly on a variety of topics
I lick the newspaper and do a shot of sawdust.
I take a saffron cliché from the closet—
hand stitched by children of the very rich—
and tie it around my thigh.

I get to my cubicle late.
A young couple is waiting.
They show me a jar of marbles. I tell them,
really what you have here is a jar of marbles
and then pull the bill from my ear.
I'm good.
Boss gives me a seven out of ten.
My coworkers paint themselves.

When the lunch whistle blows,
I slouch in my chair
and unbutton my pants.
I chew on old photographs.
They're beautiful and delicious.
After lunch I put tape on my face.

All afternoon I make animals
out of foil from gum wrappers.
I juggle sandpaper.
When it's almost time to go
Boss comes by
ties a bell around my neck
and kisses me on the Adam's apple.

Eventually I stop ringing
and hop down to the company bar.

I drink piña coladas
and condescend with other workers.
My wallet does most of the talking.

It says, *Yee Ha!*
and rides around my back pocket.

Afterwards, I'm loose shelves and compartments. I rattle
as I bring home suitcases full of bacon.
I sit on the floor of my apartment
and read the VCR manual
until it's time to go to bed.
I unzip my smile.

I'm exhausted
and sleep like Iceland.
I dream about working
in a Reykjavik fire hydrant.
I touch my tongue to frozen metal.

Agoraphobia

The stick is big but wrapped in softness.
We all go into the bathroom together.
We've taken the toilet paper so there

can be toilet paper for everyone.
But enough theory. The cosmetic muscles
do all the work. We're the kind of drunk

you write home about. Pilgrim drunk.
Drunk as a swing set. Think of a soda
machine swallowing quarters. That's us

making the most of our free time.
Presidential rain. Silver forefathers
under wigs like small obedient mammals.

They shout and drop into profit.
Furry sounds signifying refreshment.
Choice is spilt. Then quiet as ice.

We The People call it pop.

Rescue Excerpts

1. The rescue party was too enthusiastic as evidenced by antiquated rescue tools: a heavy grappling hook, snow shoes, group whistling as a way to establish that everything was going according to plan. Perhaps it's just adrenaline, I thought. But it didn't wear off.

2. The too regular opening and closing of one faded, very large and closely guarded map. When the map was open, we held our hands to it for warmth. When the map was folded, rectangle upon thickening rectangle, it was a cellar door. And which side of the door were we looking at?

3. "Don't come after us?" she said. "What in God's name are you talking about?"

4. Everyone knows that permafrost is permanently frozen ground.

5. They say that if you are lost at sea, birds are a sign of land. But we were not lost at sea, and I did not see even a single cloud that looked like a bird.

6. There are so many words in the English language for a ridge that winnows to a crumbling point. I find it annoying that you keep using only those two words: cliff and love.

7. Every one of us wanted one of us to be critically injured or killed. A bloodletting to cure. Until that happened, this was not serious. We were not serious.

8. We found them alive. We found them barely alive. We found them alive and well. We found them exhausted and frightened, but alive. We never found them. They found us. We found each other. We finally found each other.

9. The sun does stranger things.

10. There are moments in every drawn-out rescue where the rescuers blame the lost, and the lost blame the rescuers. At these times, the line between the two groups muddles. The lost want nothing more than the capacity, resources, and sense of purpose that searching brings. Often, the lost ransack their clothing and dwindling foodstuffs looking for any clue to the rescuers whereabouts. The rescuers insist that it is they themselves who are nowhere to be found.

The Man Who Hates You

The man who hates you sports a violent coiffure,
a sycophant's cravat, and doesn't know
what's good for him.

Once, he called your mother feeble and licked her face.
Another time, he pointed at your father's groin
and laughed.

When you're not around, he objectifies your lover; unleashes his
sugar tongue and disaster rears
its crinoline head.

When he sleeps, biblical insects steep out of his open mouth.
He dreams of his long fingernails defacing the moonlight;
he is both a writer and a critic.

He billows like a steam engine. He's Latinate ad nauseam.
He's slang-proof and the author of everything
horrifyingly pronounceable.

Empathy

There is a man's head inside my father's freezer. All my life I've seen his sockets, candied over with frost, on my way to the meat and the ice cream. The head says nothing and his silence gives me the courage to be silent.

There is also a woman's head, shrunken down, in a jar on my father's desk beside the mints. She floats in liquid the color of a dirty martini. It's morbid to think of this woman's head as an ancient olive. (I have never been able to eat or drink in front of other people.)

I never tell anyone this, but I think of this man and this woman as my disembodied parents. They are like magnets keeping me upright. They say nothing and I say nothing.

They taught me that a man's smile is a predatory bird. They taught me that a man's face is the surface of an ocean. And every man is an ocean. They tell me this over and over and over again.

Polysomnogram

The sleep study participant is allowed only Kung Fu movies
and dreams of snatching a stone from the master's hand,
the five point palm exploding heart technique.
The cognitive dissonance of subtitles comforts no one.

The grant money is long spent and still the subject moves
so delicately in and out of moonlight. If there were a building,
she would suddenly be on top of it. If there were a river,
she would wear it like a hat while breathing through a reed.

The sleep patterns prove nothing, but the data is elegy:
How a body can be an orchid, blade after blade.
The line graph is thin mist. The mind knows many styles.

Swashbuckle

The sun drags your shadow from your body
and flies it like crossbones.

Shame

A boy in the sky destroys Chicago
with a tiny bag of pretzels.
A boy on the ground sinks and unsinks

a velvet rope's lonely fang
into and out of its eyelet.
Boys, you can't live with them.

Memory's lung and wing
conflate: dove in a ribcage.
I know why the razor wire sings.

I don't know why she throttled the guy.
Things regained in translation.
Piloting and smiling

veins. The repetitious sunshine
arrives in the a.m. in packets of
physics, sweeter than the spines

of planes. The flames on muscle
cars and the hearts on arms
are no match for the names

on small recording devices.

Simile

My favorite t-shirts are like battered screen doors clinging to hinges.
Che Guevara flickers like a mirage.
Emerging from a fog of thread,
Marvin Gaye wears a shiny smile like a butter knife.

I want my t-shirts to perform
the difference between ideology and commodity.
Scratch that. I want my t-shirt to be *like* the difference.
Ok, so nothing is really like anything else.

Do me a favor: Next time you see someone
with a ratty, old Marvin Gaye on their chest,
press your ear against the likeness as if it was a seashell.
(You'll want to ask permission first.)

Get the go-ahead and then listen carefully
for Marvin's voice lolling but muffled, as if behind a curtain,
as if trapped behind the literal and the metaphorical,
the owner's soft bass drum heart keeping time:

I've been really trying, baby.

Giving

The thought that counts is going to count to ten.
Then there's going to be trouble.

More generous than a space ship, we're on
top of technology like pornography.

We spangle our figments in the discount sun.
We are the sheriff of double town.
We put our last dollar down where our mouth is.

Receiving

We put our heads together and made a monster.

This is not an other story. We are the villagers
when the villagers are waving our fire.

Fatigue

So much liquor to tamper
the mouthy night.

Chatter muffled slowly;
numb ceremony
(something tortured, something true).

Thin hum
like a bright blanket, barely
covering. Reticent secret,
why are your clothes so loud?

Bees

Beat a cow to death.
Put sage leaves under the corpse.
Wait.

When bees appear
collect as many as you want into a jar.
The number you gather describes your fear.

Take your jar of bees,   Stinger
your jar containing a bee,   Flower
or your empty bee jar,   Buzz
and show it to someone you love.   This could be
Your explanation describes your fear.   A field of whatever

Let the bees suffocate.   Thorax
Label the jar appropriately.   Hive
For example: Compound eyes

dead invisible bees.   This might be
                                                          A still life
                                                          With honey

Leave the jar to be found
in a place of your choice
with a poem of your choice.
These choices describe your fear.

Medicinal

How muscular nurses with weepy needles rouse doctors
from post-diagnosis bliss is anyone's guess.
I'll guess knock-knock joke, you guess prestidigitation,
and then we'll have to guess again.

The good fluid marries the bad fluid.
The paperwork eddies in proper channels peopled
with people reading all makes of junk over tuna fish lunch.

And if you hate them with all of your t-shirt,
I will love you surrealistically
in the supply closets of this teaching hospital.

Wrap me in gauze. Harness me with stethoscopes
because the interns need to see this.
This is how you specialize.

This is how you make a ward out of tongue depressors.
This is how you make money selling free samples.
This is how you perch and angle televisions
above the patience.

And this is how you close your eyes; imagine embers
dimming under the log of you, all ambulances
switching off their lights.

Balance of Power

Supreme Court Justices are hand-picked like the finest coffee beans.
In chambers they slam and slam their gavels. Always heavily
made-up, eyeliner and foundation. They drive small cars
that they trick-out to drag against other judges on secret weekends.

Supremos (as they like to be called) mull over their bench persona.
They are wrestlers on the top rope. They sit in the nose-bleeds
at arena rock shows testing their lighters against a variety of wind.
They are not allowed to intermarry.

Dissent is a high diver and a high diver is shorn for splash.
A brilliant opinion is referred to as a sugar rush.
Three in a row and you have to be Chief Justice and ride shotgun.
You get a fancier flare gun. Retirement is not a choice.

Retirement is an unconscious state. What you or I might call mystical.
What basketball players call the zone. Time slows down
to allow for deliberate movements, precise aim. Flare guns because
they are international symbols of beauty and desperation.

If I See You Tonight

There will be a sleepy man growing a gun out of his forehead.
I dreamt everyone was a cocoon full of birds.

He will be a ghost in a fedora, and you will choose
his sideways face, his marital tooth.

I dreamt everyone's birds were the color of their shoes.
The hat will also be a turntable

spinning one of several ways we say sorry.
I dreamt everyone's shoelaces were worms.

Up and down, fists switch twice to bump knuckles lovingly.
Because this is the way we shake hands in the city.

America Prefers Ventriloquism to Mime

America loves the twin
with the saucy lip
thinking outside
the invisible box.

America is
no fan of white face
and doesn't believe
the rope
describing the heaviness
of nothing.

A joke routine
and thrown voice: because
someone's got your name
and they're wearing it out.

America smiles
at a clammy hand
smuggled up a spine,
a small boy
straddling a thigh.

The conflation
of therapy and comedy.

The desire to own
the steamer trunk
in which Americana sleeps,
in which Americana sharpens,
in which Americana weeps.

Soft, delicate gloves:
the calling card
of the hit man.

Crowd Theory

Niebuhr said, groups tend to be more immoral than individuals.
He was sad in the bathtub when he said that.

He wanted to carve it into pews with his pen knife
like a child might, but he was not a child.

Instead, he dug his fingernails into the hard soap
until there were so many moons.

Method

We were discussing last century's dictators.
We were ranking them from best dresser to easiest.

Pol Pot is the size of a boom box and rides
a French bulldog like nobody's business.

We knew we didn't know what we were talking about.
We knew we had a winner on our heavenly hands.

Lullaby

The power went out and that was the end of their electric crush.
The crush was love becoming radiation:
delicious, delicious placebo.

Or, at least, that is how they sang it to kids by candlelight,
flipping a dead switch fast enough
to simulate rain.

They would sing: *It is always evening in a poorly lit apartment.*
And it is always a poorly lit apartment in my heart.
The kids loved that song.

What is an apartment? What is a heart?

An apartment is a small house sometimes in the sky.

A heart is the brain in your chest
on which you grow
a very soft spot.

Zoo Poem

I. Introduction

Whoops is the mother of invention.
Necessity is a bad mommy. The illegible shopping
list is alphabetical rain. I have flagrant cholesterol
because I would like to live in cheese.

Somewhere on this list is the death threat I sent myself: *camembert.*
I'm not scared. Don't make me flex my vegetarian muscles.
Don't say I bake the saddest croutons of childhood,
don't say I serve indigestible roughage.

II. Theme

Not so secretly, this is a poem about mortality.

III. Exploration of Theme Terminology

Let's say "fear of death" is the largest stuffed animal in FAO Schwarz.

Naturally it's a panda ("exotic," mythically friendly, but really vicious).
As you know, the panda (real, not stuffed) is virtually extinct, except in zoos.
Let's call these zoos "poems." Let's say anything can be a poem.

(Notice that I didn't say "anything *is* a poem.") This is a "for instance."

IV. Recapitulation

I'm thinking of a word beginning with x.
Is it: a) excrement   b) xylophone   c) exhume   d) exercise   e) all four

V. Coda

Post-shopping and I've forgotten several things.

Things on the list, things not on list,
things not in the grocery store.

These things
reveal or don't reveal themselves gradually, like artichokes.

Neruda has a poem about an artichoke
getting dressed up as a warrior.

Its armored skirts, its going to market,
its getting in adventures.

It's not his best poem.
I'm more into his political stuff.

Looking Forward to Leaving

The morning is trapped in a mason jar and nothing can save it.
Not blatant, nostalgic winking, not olive cream cheese
and a perfect heirloom tomato. Here a mild earthquake,
there a mild earthquake, everywhere a mild earthquake.

From procrastination's onomatopoeia inbox of sexual cliché:
Baby you're oh so attachment.
Baby you're oh so contains non-secure items.
Who's been a bad virus?

The afternoon goes straight to slow hell's pastel Easter egg basket.

Later, the downtown is armed with hackneyed neon.
It is surrounded by a forest of witty coasters
and decadent lagers that grab your tongue like a doctor.

But I don't care. I'm going to buy the biggest diet coke
I can drink and drive with. I'm going to put The Pixies in
the tape deck. I'm going to wind around
                                        morning's forehead
                                                        like a Möbius strip.
It's going to kick ass and be the opposite of Jack Kerouac.

Prime Directive

City people are not allowed to be bored and so yearn
for the expansive country. Country people,
with their incandescent ennui, long for a city they see
on channel after channel.

Thank your lucky stars it is not possible to be anywhere right now.
Unrequited landscape is more persuasive than caffeine.
Besides, city people are plot driven, and country people
are theme driven.

What happens next is: The more things change
the more they maintain shame.

For example, everyone wants to believe Rimbaud
left Paris to run guns in Africa.
It reminds everyone of their punk rock childhood.
Get shot, lose a leg, die in your sister's arms;
from country to city to country to city…

Go ahead and abandon your wanderlust mythology,
see what happens.

1. It was important to all of us to find just the right implement with which to write messages in the sand. We decided to rip a long plank off of a crate that washed up onto the beach. Some of us thought the crate came from a cruise ship (the optimists). Others thought the crate was from a pirate ship (the pessimists). Obviously we sharpened the plank so that it had a writing end and a non-writing end. We dubbed it "the ugly stick," which we hoped would prevent coveting.

2. The crate was empty. And from that seemingly innocuous fact, two philosophies were born.

3. The days are warm and pleasant, and the nights are warm and pleasant. On the very first night we gathered driftwood for a fire that we never needed. We built the fire because we were bored.

4. We eat a lot of wild rice. Wild rice is actually a grass. We sleep a lot. We sleep a lot because we are scared, bored, and lonely. We rarely sleep because we are sleepy from eating too much of the rice. Nevertheless, we often refer to sleeping as dieting.

5. Saltwater is good for the skin. Saltwater is good for the skin. Saltwater is good for the skin. Saltwater is good for the skin.

6. Pessimist: "Do you think the eye patches and rum are on the bottom of the ocean?"
Optimist: "Do *you* think the ship's Activities Coordinator is resourceful enough to make
do without?" Etc.

7. You have seen so many narratives depicting the "stranded on a deserted island predicament" that it is nearly impossible to control yourself. Though I loathe easy dichotomy, it is basically true that our behaviors fall into one of two categories. There are the people who try to resist behaving like someone they've read about, seen on television or in a movie, and there are the people who embrace these roles.

8. Someone wrote: PIGGY LOVES THE PROFESSOR MUST DIE. They wrote this perpendicular to the shoreline, so the incoming tide erased the message one letter at a time.

9. When you lose the ability to distinguish between sunburn and rash, you are in real trouble. You are delusional, and those delusions stem from an insatiable loneliness.

10. There are no cameras in the trees. Light swims through the thin canopy easily. There are plenty of birds to eat. They are without guile, simple to kill and prepare. There are no cameras in the trees.

Ars Poetica

There was a brief time during high school when huffing computer cleaner was the thing to do. Brief, I suppose, because although we could not yet afford anything more expensive than weed, we would soon be able to. Also, it was stupid, even for high school. One time, Ricky Mitchell hit it between periods outside the gym. He ran full sprint into a concrete wall. He got up, and he ran full sprint into the wall again, tossing several teeth. Then he passed out and pissed himself—a urine cloud drifting over the front of his acid-washed. It was, hands down, the funniest thing that ever happened in the history of the world. A few years later, I heard that Rick Mitchell was shot and killed by a cop in Detroit.

In *The Wealth of Nations*, Adam Smith asserted that human greed would be held in check by our need for social acceptance. I have no idea whether this is true or not.

The End of Stray Media

I was dead and then I wasn't is how I describe
the entire genre of film that begins with a slow pan
out from something incomprehensible to oh
that's what that is: sad neon in a snowstorm.

When the video store dies, as die it must, we lose
the tactile experience of browsing
and a need to collect which is architectural.
Some won't believe it if they can't stack it toward the sky.

Also, some have a previous distrust of information
that disregards walls: firefighters and apparitions.
This is not a plea to reverse the irreversible;
tomorrow thrashing against the glass.

Don't Beat a Dead Horse

I came upon a dead horse. "This is a violent land with little time for repetition," it said. "Make use of my enormous lungs. Build a little prison out of my rib cage. Race me." The dead horse was inconsolable. It must be hard in a small town in the age of the pickup truck. "The stars are so beautiful tonight like distant fence posts." There is a moment right before a horse decides to kick. The flies were thick and dark as jam. The smell coming from the dead horse was wrong. "The moon," it whispered. "I could eat it." The dead horse had a point maybe. I moved upwind and relaxed a little. The horse went on about the stars and the moon. It died a little more, it died a little less.

Sociology

They painted hummingbirds and roses on their gas masks—
that's how you knew they were a family.

Their voices caramelized in the chamber, their faces
filtered through memory.

They called each other *gift horse*, changed their minds
about romance and what it means to be a villain.

Winds filled with infinitesimal glass, only mushrooms grew
in the dead shade of what it must have felt like.

Little City Shame

Dear Crying Shame—

I learned a new palindrome: was it a bat I saw?

My hands were birds hiding in the (d)ark
and I woke up like light, empty of breath.

This month I believe in the current
crackling along wet wires.
Dizzy, ornate highways that surround us
like a motherboard.

May: cold then warm then cold
weather teasing in circuit.
May is the cruelest hangover.

***

I went up and down the little mountain
as if it was my first escalator.

As if I was eight years old and unsupervised
inside a children's book.

At the top, I sat beside the ash pit
among crushed empties.
This month, I believe
in the commercialized hiss.

This month I believe in giving up.
The crown of trails snake out and back in:
my medusa, my mirror, my stone.

The maples are invasive
and taking over—nothing finds them tasty.
Nothing finds them delicious.

This nature is in need
of some other disruption.

I learned a new palindrome: Won't lovers revolt now?

Dear Crying Shame—

In summer's humid tantrum the air licks everything incessantly.
Morning's engine overheats and citizens
become hiccups freckling noon.

Evening's gossip gets chaotic in the trees.
Cicadas make the tacky dusk scream.
Tepid liquor cracks ice.

The college kids get a happy kind of stupid in their yard
before becoming amorous pairs; clumsy limbs
working up lather.

Idle hands are the make-out-artist's chiaroscuro.

Tomorrow balloons with disinformation. Data flaps towards
sundown's lewd pink rip like a flightless bird;
everywhere evolution's remnants
do their strange, sad dance.

This is what life does: parcels out the silly
memory of similar motion.

I feel like I've already said everything. Description dances badly.
Here peels syllables off the ripe night. Imagination leaves;
the nothing grows; sound singing out to its twin.

Boredom is what privilege does to ward
off the future's masculine anatomy.
I am no great lover of chronology.

Dear Crying Shame—

Funny thing. The other day I thought the outskirts
were on fire, but it was only sunset
settling into my line of sight.

Frankly, between the cool days and good bourbon,
the ice cubes don't stand a chance.

The evenings are a blur, the season's leisure
uncomfortable; I feel suburban,
but only because I've never lived there.

It's gotten to the point where all the pills
in the world don't add up to a sky
I feel like spilling my drink over.

I keep thinking about those autumn days, years ago,
when we'd easily stumble down to the river;
our hyper-active sense of America.

What was it you used to say?

"The only pitch worth throwing is a fastball
when they know it's coming."

I want that back, whatever it was, not because
I want it, but because this isn't working.

I've forgotten how words and stories add up separately.
I'm still looking for an aftermath
to disappointment.

There's a moment in novels when everything goes
denouement, when what can't be taken back
gets salvaged from a sense of regret
and becomes a sense of fate.

It's stupid, but I don't know how to stop, and I don't know why
I'm telling you this. I guess it's because I hope
you recognize the sentiment.

I'm wondering if you feel it too.

Did we slip up? Was it inevitable? Were we so determined not to
get washed into the tightly scripted shore that we floated out
beyond our ability to recognize horizon?

Dear Crying Shame—

I would never say I'm *not* a spy.
I would say I agree with Alfred Hitchcock's
impossible criteria for crystallized memory:

The hills sleepwalk, their beards are sweet disguises digesting the wind:
the way victims smother in bad cinema, the way awkward
dancers get down to funk at weddings
all across this fine country of ours.

Seventeen hours driving from plains to mountains.
Along the way (and what isn't?):

rural, tape deck narrative
and urban sentence-level hypochondria.

It's hard to resist summarizing fathers.

Myriad disappearances into George Washington.
The pregnant silences good as any cherry tree.

All identities are mistaken identities.

Dear Crying Shame—

Conjugated death, prepositional death: You have to rearrange yourself
in order to see the world living posthumously, as you do,
behind the palmetto: sunset of rust: the steep
curve of subject.

Ditch water where mosquitoes breed.
Glass after glass of burnt earth.

When the super volcano underneath us goes, finally, status epilepticus;
when lava gets us, or carbon dioxide sneaks from lakes and palms
our lungs like coins, the sad hills touching like zombie thighs;

I want to believe this is not a view of the story
from the sky.

Dear Crying Shame—

I'm going to talk about the sky again.
(This is what love has done for me lately.)

I swept bits and chunks of glass until I could say *palace*.
Claws of light scratching at the pleases.
A range of mistakes singing to be gathered away.

How easily a center drawn from edges.
Nothing and everything calm at the eye, as they say.

This must be the dearly that belongs to the missed
and not to the beloved. This must be salt
owed the well-rubbed wound.

Blue given too easily to evening and what happens
after the country's redundant love of debauchery and grease?
Debauchery and grease, of course.

These shards are not petals. These shards
masquerading as landscape.

Yellow took easily to noon and regret's heavy, savvy
tangle. And the sky, because I said I would say,
was a gorgeous blue pancake.

Dear Crying Shame—

Death as a tense switch trick?
Think of a roadside porcupine: cute, quills, rigor mortis.
What is happening? What was happening? What will be happening?

The dead leave us like jars of change poured out onto a table.
They leave us like sound. They leave us trite: wings
 and dirt. They leave us worse, worst.

There is no such thing as nonsense. There is invoking it: its opposite. There is the
progressive and the passive. There is saying
and there is being.

There is saying, *there are no words*. And there is being this lack.
This is made. That is made. There is a scratch on the record
where the needle skips.

Dear Crying Shame—

Several things have happened since you left: The town found its death
without you, buckling gently and piecemeal—buildings easing
into themselves, their soft rot, like old men slouched down
in their chairs. Your absence implied a violence
which gathered like weather.

Kids in the park wouldn't play; they milled around in packs like architects.
At the crossroads, in the crosshairs, language pushed its luck.
(You could hear it during the riot act, saying *fuck*.)
Now a bright cry reddens every rain drop
that stops to kiss this town.

When things went to pieces, some of the pieces went missing: screen, aria
phosphorescence, blue, curve, foil, alchemy… For a while, every sky
was an exploding song. Our song. Then collective memory left
and came back romantic like a rickshaw
or a sharp stick.

Now memory festers under a pile of fancy extras. For example, the moon
is a mnemonic device reminding me of money. It wasn't always.
Remember how we loved to tie your red scarf to the couch
and lower ourselves down, darkness?

Big City Shame

Dear Crying Shame—

I've left the city my mouth to take apart.
The city's strange old tools and tinkering,
its ligature and flavors of luck.
Eerie tunes from ice cream trucks.

Behind half an inch thick of black paint

To   Repel   Ghosts

I live on the elbow of a beautiful cemetery.
I live in the caramel vortex of liberty.

Near the top of the bottomless
pit of sincerity, where language
leaps up like a bad dog
and my obvious dreams are:

no fare, rotting rain, a man from the train,
something angry from his pocket.

From the highest point among headstones,
revenants of the spring's gnarly grin,
its vacant sockets and perfect teeth,

swarms of afternoon children
turn out with their little fists

gripping the horns of the *y* at the end of mystery.

Dear Crying Shame—

Most mornings, my first underground act is to take my heart to the edge
of the platform, crest the track and desire up tunnel.

Shore anticipating ship. Entitled lighthouse. A surfing pose
summoning the train which arrives when the desire to commute is true.

Momentarily frozen towards the electric, this prayer
gathers adherents to its posture. How many hearts does it take?

***

What is cinéma vérité in a city of rolling cameras, in a city of rolling eyes,
in a city minus memory, if by memory we mean playback,
not roiling waves and undertow?

What is this question if it has been asked before?

***

If "   " = lightning in a cloud of punctuation.

"Our car" is packed like an unshakable idea.
"Our guy" is incandescent, singing *baby, baby, ba-by*, riding
his shining out into the open, his armor inviting heaven.

"Our train," like "our city," is "self correcting."

I remember sadness is a mangled bird. The word *blood*
looks like a dangerous place to lie down.

Dear Crying Shame—

To answer your question, it's good to have tangible things.
But I'm reminded of how a hyphen solders gestures.
The way useful accumulations snarl.
The low-price of things. The long-range strategy. The lock-down.

If it looks sexy it's a turn-on, but touch is hands-on, hands-off.
It's its own matter. As our opinions gnash we define
the non-negotiable: the mess of combination,
the power of naming things one. *We.*

Commonsense? How do you mean?

Of breaking into separateness, of finding lines that don't imply
their outside, I know little. The way punctuation slips in
tells me nothing in the middle of the night
about the middle of the night.

Dreams fidget away and away. In the movies,
we sit up like switchblades.

Dear Crying Shame—

For an hour the sky splices
one layer of evening to another
until night.

Light from windows climbing
up and up must be
a language like stars
and similarly without tongue.

The city is always facing forward.

Its height is the height of highest brightness,
its soupy black hat tips low
and rakishly.

What are anonymity and fame
doing tonight that we can't do?

Procedure and something
about the self ascribed by numbers.
Something about pens on chains.

Shapes cut away
from backdrop and biology.

We are the strangest things to be
moving with such sense of purpose.

Only the lonely, as the song goes,
mostly without words.

Glass conflating surfaces
and distance, or is that us?

Our eyes grip what they grip.

And ideas?
I'm thinking of that
first scene in *La Dolce Vita*:

A helicopter above the ruins
and soccer fields, its Christ necklace
swinging towards the sunbathing, rooftop girls.

Reflection jumping modernity's glass
face like a broom.

I'm thinking about obsessive angles,
plotted incidences so easily
and so absolutely outnumbered.

Dear Crying Shame—

When you said forever or farther I was in the shambles of glee.
But after, language congealed in luminous puddles.
I don't want anyone thinking inside/outside,
so keep this smothered in blankets:

Word around the campfire is *hermeneutic*. Word on the street
is *dispiteous*. Speaking of vocab, how is old
"now you see me, now you don't?"

Still a crushing blow to the spine? Did he ever find his way out
of that lacuna? I remember the time it hurt him
more than it hurt me just watching it.

Thinking about how that went down makes me parenthesis:
(I want to invent crime.)

About your untraceable miracle, turns out that tax bracket
comes with a solar powered conscience *and* raingear.
Messed up, right? It must be true what they say,
angel is an anagram for *glean*.

Anyway, if you hook up excuses count me to ten. I haven't panned out
since I was a bright idea riding on the ponies. Remember,
I'm only as wobbly as undying love for you.

Dear Crying Shame—

Somehow I've put the "un" in understanding. I forgot myself...
now you talk of an irrevocable split... can it be left at that:
life on the cusp, lost words accumulating towards a precipice?
J'accuse the discussion of a constellation.
C'est la vie under a bad sign.

The window slices up the outside: a cross section: evening
half-light disassembles the afternoon.
Stars begin to burn the night in place.
I seem to be capable of nothing more than overture.

And now, I'm left imagining us imagining other people forever.
I deserve my imagination, but silence is such a slippery thing.

In your absence, all ideas become things: I'm drowning
in clutter: this pile of me is not my name.
I'm sorry. Please write me a letter.

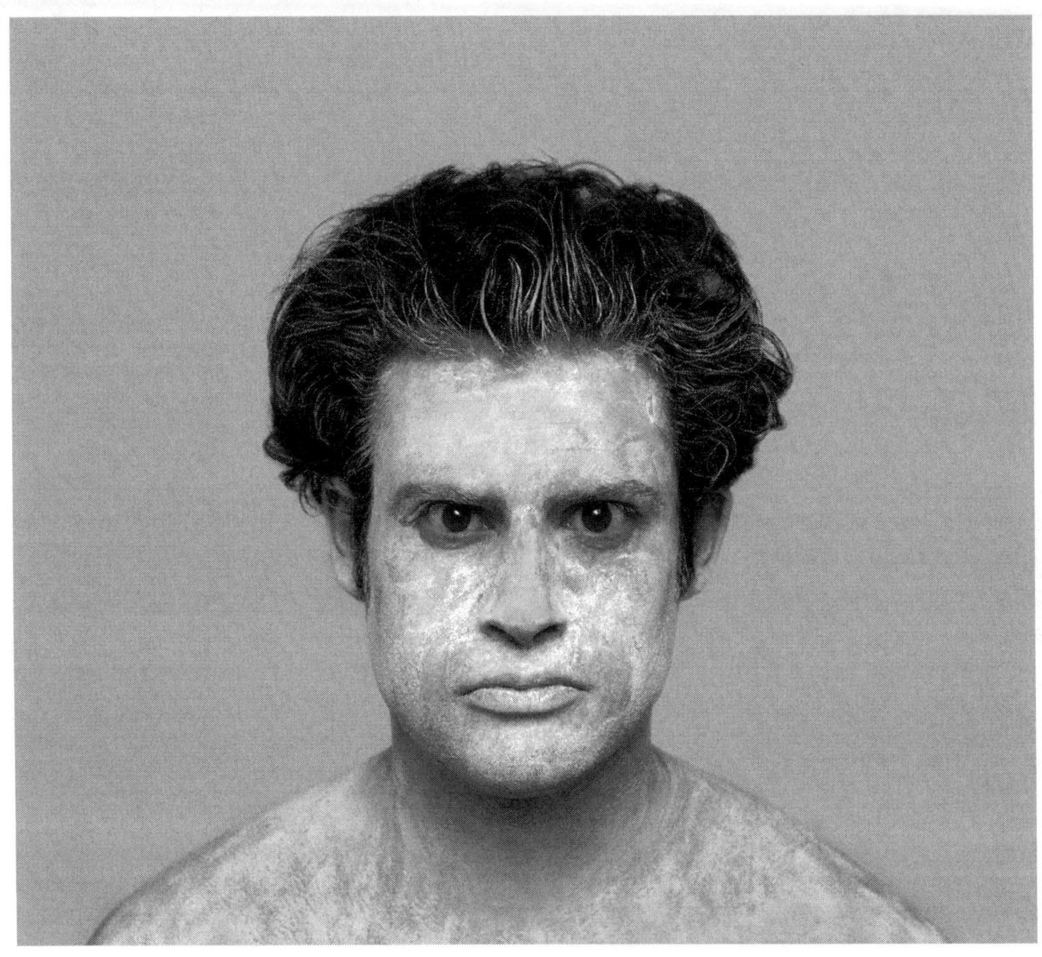

Jeffrey Morgan grew up in Fairbanks, Alaska. He is a graduate of Macalester College and Penn State University. He teaches at Borough of Manhattan Community College, and lives with his wife, poet Carla Conforto, and their daughter Stella in Kensington, Brooklyn. He can be found at thinnimbus.tumblr.com.

Made in the USA
Monee, IL
07 July 2026

56546397R00060